Deciding in Unity

*A Practical Process for
Married Couples
to Agree on Practically Everything*

Susanne M. Alexander

Deciding in Unity
Published in English in the United States by
Marriage Transformation LLC
www.marriagetransformation.com

International Standard Book Number/ISBN: 978-1-940062-00-6

© 2013 Marriage Transformation LLC (1st Ed.: June; 2nd Ed.: September). All international rights reserved for the book as a whole. No part of this book may be reproduced by any mechanical, photographic, or electronic process, or by any other means, in the form of a photographic or digital recording, nor may it be s tored in a retrieval system, transmitted, or otherwise copied for public or private use, including on the Internet, or re-sold, without the written permission of Marriage Transformation®, except by a reviewer, who may quote brief passages in a review. Translations into other languages also require permission. *Thank you for respecting this legal copyright. Your integrity with this process spreads a spirit of loving respect throughout the world and makes us very happy.*

This publication is intended to provide helpful and educational information about marriage. It is sold with the understanding that the publisher and the author are not engaged in rendering legal or clinical advice. No information, advice, or suggestions by the author are intended to take the place of directly consulting with a licensed professional if required. The author and publisher shall have neither liability nor responsibility to any person or entity with respect to any loss or damage caused, or alleged to be caused, directly or indirectly, by the information contained in this book.

Cover Design:
Nikki Vickers, nvickers23@gmail.com; www.nikkivickers.com

Cartoons: License to Use from Dave Coverly, Randy Glasbergen, and Catherine Hosack

Publisher's Note and Acknowledgements

The experiences shared in this book were provided with permission from clients and workshop participants, or they are composites from the experiences of married couples. Some identifying details have been changed. No attribution for them is provided to protect privacy and confidentiality.

The author and publisher are very grateful for the generous sharing from these couples. We welcome others to submit their experiences to us through email at susanne@marriagetransformation.com. Please include a note of permission to use them in a future book.

Marriage Transformation also sincerely appreciates the excellence of our editorial review team, which included some couples who shared their experiences. Our books serve others better because of your helpful service.

Marriage Transformation® is an educational service company dynamically empowering individuals, couples, and professionals to gain knowledge and skills for creating happy, unified, and lasting character-based marriages.
www.marriagetransformation.com

Table of Contents

Introduction		1
1	Understanding the Process of "Couple Consultation"	2
2	Managing What Gets in the Way	10
3	Applying Love to the Process	17
4	Applying Character to the Process	20
5	Including Character Affirmations	29
6	Building Understanding: Physical Arrangements	34
7	Building Understanding: Your Mix of Feelings	38
8	Building Understanding: Sharing and Listening	43
9	Building Understanding: When It's Difficult	50
10	Consulting in Unity	56
11	Putting the Process into Action	62
12	Engaging in More Practice	67
End-Note: Coming Full-Circle Back to Unity		71
About the Author and Publisher		73

Symbols in the Book

 = Actions for Couples to Take

 = The Experiences of Couples

Introduction

I love being faced with a puzzling situation and finding good solutions. I have often questioned the assumption that a couple has to fight or that conflict is normal in a marriage. Of course, issues will always come up, and you realize you have different feelings, opinions, and perspectives. However, it's possible to learn how to share these with love and respect. It is possible to work through a problem-solving process harmoniously and come to an agreement without damaging your relationship. It's crazy to have to do marriage-repair over and over after trying to make decisions together (even though it can be fun at times to "make-up" after a problem is solved!).

Making decisions well requires engaging in the process as equals, with full respect for each other. The model of one spouse dominating the other no longer works. For the best decisions, you both need to fully participate in the collaborative process. Achieving this is a "work-in-progress" for most marriages.

Another aspect of marriage that vitally relates to decision-making is that of unity. How can you build unity in your marriage so your decision-making goes well? How can you share differing opinions without personally attacking each other? How can you be companions on the same team throughout the process? What helps and what interferes with carrying out a decision you make together? How can your couple decision-making actually increase the harmony in your marriage?

Character also affects your decision-making, because it influences all your behaviors. For years I've helped people understand how respect, compassion, truthfulness, and many other character qualities affect relationships and marriages in particular.

There is no 1-2-3 or A-B-C method for making decisions that will work for every couple in every situation. Every individual has a unique personality and character, and every marriage is unique. Every family has its own circumstances and needs. There are, however, essential principles, approaches, and skills that may universally apply, and you can use them to the best of your ability. As you follow the process of Couple Consultation presented in this book, you will build a marriage full of love, character, understanding, and unity.

Susanne M. Alexander, Relationship and Marriage Educator

Chapter 1
Understanding the Process of "Couple Consultation"

You will likely be relieved and happy to know that many communication skills you have already learned in your marriage will help with making decisions. Although each chapter will suggest some practices that may be new to you, you probably already have some skills that contribute to success.

You will begin by learning below some new words and concepts associated with couple decision making.

UNITY: The Beginning, Middle, and End

Unity is vital in maintaining healthy and happy marriages. When you are unified, making decisions works more smoothly and increases your harmony. Unity is often the *means* to solving problems and reaching agreements. Unity then helps you effectively carry out decisions you have made.

When you value unity, you consciously look for points of agreement, harmony, and attraction. You work together to build a strong foundation of oneness, love, commitment, and cooperation. Unity is not sameness—you both bring a diversity of perspectives and approaches and respect how they contribute toward the solution. You feel and act as if you are on the same team, and you demonstrate a spirit of goodwill toward each other. You know that what you create together is better than anything you could develop separately.

You seek out what is best for the integrity and prosperity of your marriage and family, always considering the well-being, rights, and responsibilities of each person involved. When one person is injured, you are all injured; what comforts or helps one, helps all; and what honors one, honors all. When unity is a vital and foundational operating principle for your marriage, you experience stability and provide a hopeful model for peaceful families and communities.

GENERATE THE ☼ LIGHT ☼ OF UNITY:
LOVE + CHARACTER + UNDERSTANDING = UNITY

UNITY = ☼ LIGHT ☼
Making decisions in harmony is one way to create
the light of unity

The chapters that follow will explain these concepts in more depth.

DISUNITY: Disruptions Along the Way

You might also add the word "disunity" to your marriage vocabulary. Any time you are feeling disconnected from each other, look for what may have caused disunity between you. Here are some causes of disunity in relationships:

- A promise not kept
- Unkind words
- A judgment made quickly without considering the facts
- Stubborn insistence on an opinion or specific solution, with rejection of the spouse's views

DISUNITY = ● DARKNESS ●
Insisting that you are right and your spouse is wrong
causes disunity

Disunity in your marriage arises from negative and destructive words and interactions. Research shows that some of the behavior patterns below are the most damaging to a marriage.

Spouse A: Criticizes the personality or attacks the character of Spouse B; example, "You are so irresponsible."

Spouse B: Reacts defensively, blaming Spouse A; example, "I am not! You are always picking on me!"

Spouse A: Shows contempt for Spouse B through body language, sneering, sarcasm, or patronizing or self-righteous

Deciding in Unity

comments; example, "You're such an idiot! "Can't you do anything right?"
Spouse B: Withdraws to avoid communication, thereby stonewalling and shutting Spouse A out

(Based on John Gottman, PhD, and Nan Silver, *The Seven Principles for Making Marriage Work*, Ch. 2)

Further examples of destructive statements:

- You are so irresponsible with the bills.
- You never listen to me.
- You are a lousy parent.

Any character attack, severe criticism, or stubborn insistence on one's own opinion will cause the darkness of disunity. If these behaviors occur during decision-making, it will not be possible to have a positive outcome.

Persistent disunity in a marriage results in conflict, usually quarrelling or actually battling with each other. A couple acts and speaks in strong opposition to each other, disputing with what each other says, which leads to bitter discord.

Increasing Unity = Decreasing Conflict

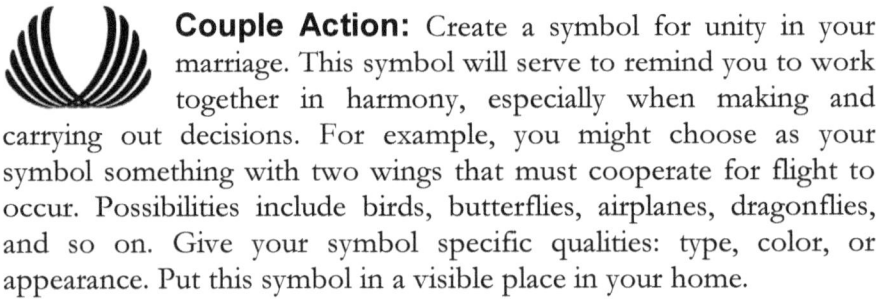

Couple Action: Create a symbol for unity in your marriage. This symbol will serve to remind you to work together in harmony, especially when making and carrying out decisions. For example, you might choose as your symbol something with two wings that must cooperate for flight to occur. Possibilities include birds, butterflies, airplanes, dragonflies, and so on. Give your symbol specific qualities: type, color, or appearance. Put this symbol in a visible place in your home.

Understanding Couple Consultation

Throughout the rest of this book, unified couple decision-making will be referred to as "Couple Consultation". As with "unity," and "disunity," this phrase will become a regular part of your marriage vocabulary. Increasing unity in your marriage is worth the effort! You will increase your understanding of Couple Consultation and your skills with each chapter. For now, it will help to begin with a short description of what it is.

Characteristics of Couple Consultation:

- Collaborative communication takes place between two (or more) people before making decisions or taking actions
- Focus is on seeking to determine truth and understanding of each other, often clarifying your thoughts, views, preferences, requests, goals, beliefs, and feelings as well as sharing any factual details
- Both spouses contribute equally to the process, sharing information, offering opinions for consideration, and seeking to understand and gain new insights from different—and even apparently clashing—perspectives
- Each spouse flexibly and open-mindedly receives new information and makes shifts to incorporate new understandings
- Purposes and directions are harmonized in reaching a mutually-agreeable decision about what is best to do or not do, often something new neither thought of before
- Decisions and plans carried out in unity that do not turn out well may be quickly corrected through further Couple Consultation

> "...[C]onsultation must have for its object the investigation of truth. He who expresses an opinion should not voice it as correct and right but set it forth as a contribution to the consensus of opinion, for the light of reality becomes apparent when two opinions coincide."
> ~ 'Abdu'l-Bahá, *The Promulgation of Universal Peace*, p. 72

The world is moving at a very fast pace, and people often want "quick tips" and "simple steps" for magical change. Once you learn to use Couple Consultation, you will often be able to carry it out quickly. Learning this skill, however, will be a gradual, experiential, and dynamic process. The more you incorporate it into your life, the more natural it will feel. And, no matter how swiftly you learn to carry it out, there will always be times when you need to slow down the pace. This will give you enough time to determine adequate facts, sort out and express feelings, and allow for an organic process of resolving an issue.

Couple Reflection: Before you begin learning a new pattern of behavior, it can be helpful to gain clarity on what is currently happening. As you discuss the questions below, make notes of what you already do well and what behaviors you wish to improve.

1. What types of problems are easy for us to manage together?
2. What types of decisions are more difficult for us to make together?
3. What feelings seem to be present in each of us when we have a decision to make?
4. What current patterns in our communications may need to change for effective Couple Consultation to occur? For example:
    o Becoming defensive when stating an idea or opinion?
    o Being stubborn about opinions during discussions?
    o Acting judgmental about ideas?
5. What would we like our Couple Consultation process to look like?

Couple Equality

Couples everywhere are learning how to work together with mutual respect and equal voices in their marriages. However, you may still have expectations for how men and women communicate and make decisions. This may trip you up in Couple Consultations. You will need to watch out for times you may slip back into unequal expectations or behaviors. Your willingness to try new behaviors is vital. Establishing equality in a marriage is often not easy, and equality is a complex subject beyond the scope of this book. However, because equality contributes to effective Couple Consultation, it is included briefly below.

Equality is working as a team in your marriage, honoring each other as worthy human beings. It is a balance of power that helps you respect one another as true partners. You support and encourage one another, helping both of you to develop to your fullest potential as you build a strong marriage and family together.

Both of you have the opportunity to seek education and employment. You are equally responsible for participating in your family and community, and you honor one another's contribution. Equality does not mean you make the same choices or that your roles are identical. You have different physical abilities and skills, which allow you to contribute in different ways. Although, you are aware of gender traditions and stereotypes, you avoid making thoughtless choices based on them.

Together you consult, make decisions, share responsibilities, and learn new skills as needed to increase balance and harmony in your home. You do not treat each other as superior or inferior. Even when one has more expertise than the other in a particular area, the power to act is shared. You do not give one another unwelcome assistance or advice. You consult together and reach mutual decisions about your lives, marriage, family, and work, always considering what is best for all. You both have the opportunity to contribute during Couple Consultations, and you carefully listen to one another's points of view. You each have a body, mind, heart, and soul worthy of equal respect.

> "Consultation is a method for finding out the truth, solving problems, deciding on the best course of action, preventing difficulties, and generating new ideas and plans. It is a tool for equitably sharing power and decision making between two or more people."
> ~ K. Khavari and S. Khavari, *Creating a Successful Family*, p. 68

One Couple's Experience: We have been married for about 12 years. Most evenings, we eat together in our home with our two children, who are now ages 10 and 7. From the time they were quite young, we started the practice of settling them with quiet activities after dinner. This gives us time to retreat to a quiet spot in our home. We share the events of our days with one another and consult as necessary about anything on our minds.

Our Couple Consultations often include such topics as these:

- "Between us, whose time commitments will best allow for driving the children to after-school activities this week?"
- "We have our appointment with the financial planner coming up in two weeks. What issues do we think are the most important ones for us to consult about with her? What preparations do we need to make?"
- "We are hosting this month's married couples group on Saturday evening. When will we finish up our reading assignment? How will we get the house cleaned and refreshments arranged?"
- "I'm concerned about my medical test next week, and I would be calmer with you there. Is there anything you can change in your work schedule so that you can go with me?"

Certain questions have helped us as we consult, and they seem to shorten the time required for Couple Consultation:

- What do we want to see happen?
- Does either of us have any strong preferences related to the topic?
- Are there any particular goals we are trying to meet?

We learned early on in our marriage that we both tend to be irritable and negative when we are tired and hungry. Serious talk before dinner always ended in sharp words. The children have learned that we are better parents when they give us this quiet time after dinner. We are committed to showing the children that it's possible to discuss issues without loud voices and arguing. We aren't always successful, but most of the time we are. When we are done, then we focus on the children's needs until they are in bed for the night.

 Couple Consultation Practice: What did you learn from or appreciate about this story? Is there anything you can apply in your own marriage?

Chapter 2
Managing What Gets in the Way

GENERATE THE ☼ LIGHT ☼ OF UNITY:
LOVE + CHARACTER + UNDERSTANDING = UNITY

When you begin to learn Couple Consultation, and even when you become more skillful, you will discover that sometimes it goes smoothly, and sometimes it doesn't. Being human includes not being perfect! You will learn over time what helps you prepare for Couple Consultation and what helps improve the smooth flow of the process. You will also learn about what builds unity and what causes disunity between you.

Each individual and couple has their own challenges, so this chapter cannot address every possible obstacle you may face. Some more are listed in Chapter 9, "Building Understanding: When It's Difficult". Take what you can use from the material below, and then identify other issues for you to work on individually or together.

A bond of intimacy and trust always facilitates Couple Consultations. When you are experiencing unity, it's easier to be vulnerable with each other, knowing the response to what you share is more likely to be loving. When you are feeling unified, you are less likely to be selfish or judgmental in your focus and responses, and it's easier to consider everyone involved.

Couple Reflection and Couple Consultation Practice: It will help you begin building your skill with Couple Consultation if you understand what you already do that unifies you. Individually reflect on the statements below, and then share your responses with each other.

"I feel unified with you when you/I: _____."

"I feel unified with you when we do _____ together."

Ask yourselves about being unified in your marriage:

- What is working well?

- Where do we see room for improvement?
- How can we accomplish changes?

If you are uncertain about what to improve, simply move forward with the book and gather ideas as you go.

Address Issues from the Past

As part of your personal growth journey, it is wise to address any issues from the past that might interfere with your marriage and Couple Consultations. Family or previous relationships or marriages may have left you with unresolved feelings about incidents that happened.

For example, if as a child you felt your opinion was always rejected and ridiculed, you may have a difficult time expressing yourself and believing that you matter, even in a loving marriage. If you established unhealthy communication patterns in a previous failed marriage, those patterns may re-emerge, unbidden, in your current marriage. If as a child you heard your parents fight a lot, you may do almost anything to avoid potential conflict, even in cases where conflict is not arising.

A strong emotional need for peacefulness in your home could lead you to:

- Bypass Couple Consultation and make decisions independently
- Always verbally agree with your spouse
- Hold back some of your own thoughts during Couple Consultation

Solving long-standing personal issues may require counseling or therapy. If they are not identified and addressed, however, they will continually revisit and sabotage your current attempts at Couple Consultation. You may be triggered by emotions related to the previous situations, possibly without self-awareness. Strong emotional reactions such as fear, shame, guilt, grief, and anger stemming from the past can confuse your spouse.

If you are able to identify that past events are affecting you in the present, you can use Couple Consultation to explore what is happening. For example, "When you interrupt me, I feel angry because it reminds me of how my first husband always interrupted me when we talked." You can follow that with a request, "Please allow me to finish talking before you begin." Both of you can then watch for what might awaken the distress, and diffuse or address it as it arises.

Practice Self-Respect

Many people seem to struggle with "unworthiness" today. When people feel unworthy, they often question whether they deserve respect and love. This pattern can cause you to wonder about the value of your contributions in Couple Consultations. If you withhold your thoughts and feelings, the quality of the decision-making process deteriorates. When you agree to decisions without having contributed your opinions, it will be more difficult for you to fully participate in carrying out the decisions. You will not be completely invested in the outcome. The more uncertain you are about being worthy of respect, the harder it will be for you to be engaged in all aspects of your marriage.

At the foundation of self-respect is the recognition that you are each essentially noble human beings with the ability to contribute to your marriage and in other situations. When you are in an active mode of striving to learn and improve, you will tend to produce positive results that increase your self-respect. Even if you don't quite qualify for sainthood!

Look honestly and objectively at what you are doing well. Decide where you need to focus your self-improvement efforts, but don't spiral downward with criticism and excessive focus on achieving perfection. Where there is self-respect, you can acknowledge your efforts to grow, and you become happier and better able to work with, relate to, and serve each other and others.

Stay Aware of Your Own Thoughts and Feelings

Before consulting, it is wise to reflect on your own thoughts and feelings about a topic, acknowledging any personal biases based on gender or culture. You may have layers of responses. Practices such as prayer, meditation, or journal-writing may help you calmly think through a topic and gain some insights. Having some clarity at the outset will contribute to the effectiveness of the Couple Consultation. You will also further clarify your thoughts and feelings through the process of consulting, which raises questions and ideas.

Also, pay close attention to your mood and current frame of mind. Look for any internal agitation, frustration, sadness, hunger, anger, tiredness, or other issues that may block your ability to be fully present and engaged in the Couple Consultation. Addressing these issues first can improve your experience.

You may also, at times, struggle with fear or feelings of vulnerability before and throughout the process. It takes heart-courage to share your thoughts and feelings, even when you are in a loving marriage. If you are feeling disunity in your relationship, it takes even more courage to address and find solutions to a problem. It takes practice and commitment for you to create a compassionate and safe sharing space. Criticizing or belittling each other can quickly shut off sharing. As you build mutual trust and respect, you will find it easier to share your points of view.

Do you tend to rehearse mentally and emotionally what you will say during a Couple Consultation? This may have positive benefits, helping you:

- Assess what issues are wise to bring up at this time
- Clarify your thoughts
- Calm yourself

Alternatively, rehearsing might escalate negative feelings, causing you to obsess about the problem and become attached to your own point of view. You could be experiencing a need to control what happens. Try to avoid what seems harmful, and do what is beneficial for you and the circumstances.

Assess Your Motives

An attitude of goodwill toward each other is essential for effective Couple Consultation. When you both want what is best for one another, your marriage, and your family, you will make better decisions. Your focus will be achieving understanding and making a unified and mutually-satisfying decision rather than on getting your own way.

Couple Consultation is not a contest to "win". Notice if your thoughts contain the words "I" or "me", which can reflect ego involvement, sometimes in very subtle ways. Disunity will result if either of you attempts to manipulate or force the Couple Consultation to go in a particular direction. Detach from what the outcome will be, and trust in the unity-building process underway.

> "I define connection as the energy that exists between people when they feel seen, heard, and valued; when they can give and receive without judgment; and when they derive sustenance and strength from the relationship."
> ~ Brené Brown, *The Gifts of Imperfection*, p. 19

[Note: Researcher Brené Brown has done extensive exploration of vulnerability, shame, unworthiness, and living wholeheartedly. She teaches that allowing oneself to be vulnerable to others, while maintaining respectful boundaries, can be a key contributor to building unity. You may find some of her resources useful. (www.brenebrown.com)]

Overcome Blocks

You may begin consulting together and then realize that you are experiencing limited thinking, like these examples:

- There is only one possible outcome to this discussion
- Either we do X or we do Y; there are no other options
- If we do take this action, then anything else is impossible
- If I'm right, then my spouse has to be wrong; there is no other way to look at it

Mindsets like these limit your ability to generate creative solutions. With a more open approach, you may begin to see that you each may have "right" perspectives that can contribute to the outcome. You can look at the problem from multiple angles and consider many solutions. You can ask, "What might be possible in this situation?"

 **One Couple's Experience:** The most productive way that I have found in my marriage for building closeness and learning about each other is practicing Couple Consultation together. We help each other share freely with one another. Through consulting together, we have learned each other's weaknesses and strengths and how to help one another. However, we didn't start out being that skillful.

Before I married my current husband, I had a serious relationship with another man. It took me a long time to see how his words toward me eroded my self-respect and self-confidence. He would say things like "You don't have a useful thought in your head," or "Where did you come up with that stupid idea?". I sought counseling after the relationship ended, which helped me heal and also prepare for a new relationship and for marriage.

In spite of the counseling help, the past still caused a challenge when I entered into a close relationship with another man. Early in our marriage, I instantly tensed up when my husband and I began consulting. I was on guard, fearing that he might criticize me. Instead of paying attention to the topic and what I might say, I watched his facial expressions anxiously and listened for an insulting tone of voice. I wanted to spot any upcoming negativity, so I could run away. Obviously Couple Consultations did not go well!

Thankfully, my loving husband realized that we were going astray, and he made some helpful suggestions. "Sweetie, how about we spend time with me just holding you and telling you how much I love you before we start talking. We could even try consulting with you in my arms!" Being newlyweds, however, sometimes that turned into a distraction!

We have found, however, that holding hands or sitting knee-to-knee while we talk often helps. Sometimes he rubs the tension out of my shoulders. I've gradually built trust in his kindness and gentleness and learned to relax, listen, and participate much better.

 **Couple Consultation Practice:** What did you learn from or appreciate about this story? Is there anything you can apply in your own marriage?

Deciding in Unity

"You're getting pretty good at this stress management thing."

Couple Consultation Practice: Share with each other what may seem to block smooth interactions when you make routine decisions or when you face a more difficult situation. Consult about ways to address the issues you identify.

Note: Some marriages are affected by such serious problems such as mental illness, active addictions, or violence. Any of these could make it very difficult or virtually impossible to effectively consult. In these circumstances, it is wise to seek professional intervention and help.

Chapter 3
Applying Love to the Process

GENERATE THE ☼ LIGHT ☼ OF UNITY:
LOVE + CHARACTER + UNDERSTANDING = UNITY

Marriage is a continual process of working together as two individuals to build love and unity. It is striving for oneness. There are many books on the subject of how to understand each other and how to express love in your marriage. This chapter is simply a brief reminder of its importance and helping you see the link between love and Couple Consultation.

Couples who increase expressions of love in their everyday interactions are likely to consult more harmoniously and productively. For example, love and intimacy may build when you:

- Make coffee or prepare meals
- Water the flowers or take out the trash
- Honor an anniversary with a special gift
- Hug and kiss before going to work or when arriving home
- Rub sore feet
- Give a compliment
- Share interesting details or a funny story from your day

Love and respect help you let go of self-centeredness. You then think in terms of "What is best for us?" and let go of the need to be "right" or "superior".

When you feel loving toward one another, you consult more smoothly. When you demonstrate love and caring throughout the Couple Consultation process, you are more likely to generate unity. Loving actions during the process can include:

- Listening intently
- Providing positive feedback
- Sharing affection (as appropriate)
- Staying conscious of one another's well-being
- And more....

Deciding in Unity

◯ **Couple Consultation Practice:** Identify two actions that you will each do in the coming week to help the other feel more loved. Assess the experience at the end of the week and consult about what you will keep doing.

◯ **Couple Consultation Practice:** Explore options and then agree on a loving action that you will do together before you begin consulting. After a few times of taking this action, assess whether it is increasing your feelings of love for one another. If it is not, consult and agree on a new action to take.

One Couple's Experience: We have been married for about three years and recently went through our first major crisis. For months, both of us became increasingly busy with work and community service activities.

Without really noticing, we began developing some poor habits. We rarely said, "I love you" to each other. Often we ate the evening meal on our own. We both forgot our wedding anniversary. The frequency and quality of our sexual experiences was dropping.

One evening my mother casually asked us when we planned to give them a grandchild. We just said we'd let them know and changed the topic. When we returned home, we tried to consult about the possibility of a baby and quickly ended up upset with each other. The loving connection between us had grown so weak that we had difficulty imagining bringing a child into our home! It was a major wake-up moment.

We really do love each other, and we both want to be parents, so we had to make some changes. We cut back on some of our activities, negotiated some work changes, and began going away together one weekend a month. We also sought some help to strengthen our marriage skills.

The effort to deepen our loving connection was successful, for which we are very grateful. We recently bought a house with space for children, and our first baby is on the way. We know now that maintaining our love and marriage is a high priority.

 **Couple Consultation Practice:** What did you learn from or appreciate about this story? Is there anything you can apply in your own marriage?

> "We cultivate love when we allow our most vulnerable and powerful selves to be deeply seen and known, and when we honor the spiritual connection that grows from that offering with trust, respect, kindness, and affection.
>
> "Love is not something we give or get; it is something that we nurture and grow, a connection that can only be cultivated between two people when it exists within each one of them—we can only love others as much as we love ourselves.
>
> "Shame, blame, disrespect, betrayal, and the withholding of affection damage the roots from which love grows. Love can only survive these injuries if they are acknowledged, healed, and rare."
>
> ~ Brené Brown, PhD, *Daring Greatly*, pp. 105-106

Chapter 4
Applying Character to the Process

GENERATE THE ☼ LIGHT ☼ OF UNITY:
LOVE + CHARACTER + UNDERSTANDING = UNITY

The light of character qualities shines brighter than the sun in your lives and marriage. They contribute substantially to generating unity in your marriage, and they influence the quality of your Couple Consultation process and decisions.

While strengthening character qualities is essentially individual work, improving your character also occurs through interactions with others. You can gently influence one another to practice the qualities.

There are dozens of character qualities you could each have as strengths, and many of them are listed later in this chapter. However, below are some that will especially help maintain the quality of your Couple Consultations.

1. Acceptance
2. Compassion
3. Cooperation
4. Creativity
5. Discernment
6. Encouragement
7. Flexibility
8. Moderation
9. Respect
10. Trustworthiness
11. Truthfulness
12. Wisdom

Here are definitions and details of how these 12 qualities can look within a healthy and happy marriage.

1. **Acceptance is** a deep, meaningful embracing of who someone is, as well as acknowledging that people and events are as they are or were as they were, rather than wasting time and energy trying to change people, regret the past, or influence events when it is unwise or there is no possibility of success.

Accepting one another unconditionally gives us the freedom to be ourselves physically, mentally, emotionally, and spiritually. We are free to love one another just as we are, without expecting the other to change. However, this acceptance often gives us the freedom to choose to change. As an act of love to one another, acceptance frees us to grow and develop our skills, capacities, and talents.

We understand that challenges are part of life, and we handle them without complaint and with humor and grace. Practicing acceptance assists us in being calm, patient, and forgiving of mistakes. Sometimes we are uncomfortable, frustrated, or upset in response to each other's actions or words. Acceptance helps us to understand one another better. When we talk about our feelings, we may agree to be flexible and make changes in our attitudes, speech, or behavior. Other times, we may simply choose to accept that our points of view are valid but different.

2. **Compassion is** feeling genuine concern for others and oneself, empathizing with the pain and suffering of those in difficult situations, and seeking ways to relieve their pain and ease their suffering.

Compassion in our marriage shows in our sympathetic and sincere concern and understanding for one another and also for others and their difficulties. Compassion helps us sense pain in each other's heart and life and in those close to us. This understanding helps us to act in ways that relieve this suffering, sometimes sacrificing our own needs in the process. Compassion allows us to reach out generously to comfort, listen to, or forgive one another and ourselves. We especially appreciate caring words when one of us makes a mistake or is in trouble, grieving, ill, injured, or hurt. We are compassionate in response to one another and ourselves when we express how sorry we are for what we have done. Compassion helps us to be good friends.

3. **Cooperation is** working with others in harmony to create or accomplish something that would be more difficult or impossible to accomplish by one person working alone.

With cooperation in our marriage, we fully communicate, engage in Couple Consultation, work together in harmony, and help one another as partners. We approach tasks together with a positive spirit. We deeply appreciate the cooperation we contribute to our marriage, family, and community. We share thoughts, ideas, and time, maintaining accountability for our actions but not trying to force one another to do something.

We support each other's personal goals, and we work in loving partnership toward our common goals. With cooperation, we can accomplish more together than we can separately. Sometimes this means we compromise or adjust our ideas, wishes, and expectations to accommodate those of the other, or to achieve a reasonable consensus. Cooperation helps us with finding solutions that work well and carry out decisions made in unity.

4. **Creativity is** drawing on ideas, inspiration, or imagination to develop or produce something new, including contributions and solutions that benefit others or oneself.

Our marriage is a unique and special relationship that we create together. We freely use our imaginations to keep our approach to life and our marriage interesting and invigorating. We create new and wonderful ways to enhance our love, communication, friendship, and marriage.

We generate creative ideas and make plans to carry them out. We dare to dream big and discover new ideas, possibilities, and inventions. Innovative solutions and possible resources arise in our Couple Consultations that address issues in our lives. Expressing creativity through writing, poetry, music, or art nourishes our souls. Often we can then share what we have created with others. We are creative in discovering new ways to express our thoughts and emotions to one another. We regularly add new experiences and spice to our lives.

5. **Discernment is** perceiving and understanding oneself, others, and situations accurately, deeply, and objectively, including discriminating between what is beneficial and what is harmful, without prejudice or bias.

Discernment assists us with looking at a variety of perspectives and facts and responding appropriately, honestly, and fairly to what is true and useful. We avoid being prejudiced, acting biased, or relying on stereotypes. We can then observe and listen intently and with sensitivity to determine what is real, true, and important about someone or a situation. As needed, we seek other perspectives and information. We do not take what we learn and use it inappropriately.

We consult about issues that are troubling or unclear to discern their true nature, potential solutions, and actions to take. Discernment helps us to recognize when an issue from our past is affecting us negatively in the present. This gives us the opportunity to respond to it and then put it back in the past. We observe and analyze the needs and priorities of our lives, relationships, home, work, and community.

Discernment also gives us keen perception of the blessings in our life and world. Even when others see only the negative, we can discern what is wonderful or find a hidden wisdom in it. We see things for what they are and understand them in their wider and deeper context. We can look at what is mysterious, discover its heart, and gain new knowledge and inspiration from it.

6. **Encouragement is** offering sincere, uplifting acknowledgment of the character strengths, effective actions, or good intentions of others and oneself; inspiring or assisting others and oneself to start, continue, or stop doing something; and fostering personal growth and development.

We know what is important to one another and what our plans are and then provide positive words and actions that inspire one another into courageous action. We help each other with fears and uncertainties that arise, showing confidence in one another's ability to succeed. Encouragement lifts our hearts and prompts us to try harder. Mutual encouragement brings us closer together, and we appreciate one another more.

If we ridicule or devalue each other or criticize each other's character rather than encourage personal growth, we know we are being highly destructive to our marriage. We do not compare each other unfavorably to others or take each other for granted. We acknowledge the best in one another's words and actions.

Encouragement releases positive thoughts, emotions, and creative energy in our lives. It is one of the greatest ways we help one another and sustain our marriage.

7. **Flexibility is** adjusting to life as it happens and embracing changes as needed, while remaining true to one's core values, beliefs, and appropriate priorities.

Flexibility helps us in changing plans or outcomes as needed, while remaining true to our values and beliefs. We appreciate the joys and benefits of unplanned or unexpected activities in our marriage, welcoming and celebrating the opportunity to be spontaneous. We do not get upset with the good intentions of others, even when they take us by surprise. We bend gently and choose to flow without resistance, fear, or anger with what happens in our lives. We are open to change and to one another's opinions, ideas, choices, and feelings.

We are able to be open to and appreciate new ideas, different creative options, innovative approaches, and alternative perspectives. We consider spiritual teachings, which can give us standards and guidance for being flexible about choices or firm about principles. Flexibility helps us to learn from challenges, adapt to new circumstances, change our minds, eliminate bad habits, and try new behaviors that support our marriage. It helps us to grow, change, and develop together.

8. **Moderation is** recognizing and avoiding extremes in use of time, words, actions, and other choices, to seek a balance that creates positive outcomes.

Moderation helps us with seeking the balance in various aspects of our marriage and lives. Choices in our lives are abundant. We regularly take a step back to assess our use of time, attention, and resources; consult about our priorities; and wisely choose steps toward maintaining a balanced life. We include family, work, service, and leisure in our lives, but with appropriate boundaries and priorities. Moderation helps us to have the time to share our thoughts and feelings, lowers our stress level, and allows us to be more relaxed and rested.

We handle our responsibilities with a higher level of integrity, and there is more energy for fun, intimacy, and affection. We are able to keep nurturing our marriage as one of our most important priorities. When we practice moderation, we use self-discipline, control our strong desires, and respond calmly when we experience challenges. We blend the practice of various character qualities together to achieve balance. We spend wisely, eat healthily, speak respectfully, and move through life with purpose, grace, and ease.

9. **Respect is** interacting with all people and what they value, as well as animals and the environment, in a manner that demonstrates they are worthy of fair treatment, consideration, and honorable regard.

Respect in our marriage helps us with listening to and valuing one another's thoughts, feelings, needs, boundaries, and rights. This respect contributes to the harmonious functioning of our marriage and home on a foundation of equality and making decisions using Couple Consultation. It increases our attraction to one another and our intimacy. We treat our bodies, minds, hearts, souls, beliefs, belongings, history, experiences, and home with interest, honor, dignity, care, appreciation, and consideration. We treat one another's belongings respectfully, honoring their value to the other.

We show respect for one another's spiritual beliefs and practices. We remember and acknowledge special dates, anniversaries, and other key events in our lives. Our families know we respect them because we stay in contact and seek their companionship. We take respectful care of our home and our neighborhood, and we receive respect from our neighbors in return. We follow and obey the rules, guidelines, and laws applicable to our situation. Respect makes life more peaceful and orderly for us.

10. **Trustworthiness is** handling tasks, responsibilities, possessions, money, and information reliably and honestly, thereby earning the confidence of others.

Trustworthiness allows us to have consistent confidence in one another's words and actions. We are truthful and faithful to one another. We trust that we will treat one another with respect and fairness. We keep our commitments and appropriate confidences, do not gossip or backbite, handle money with integrity and honesty, and give honorable service to others.

We rely on one another, and others rely on the promises we make together. We can be trusted to do what aligns with our values. We make choices that are for the greater good of our marriage, our family, and society. We build credibility by not acting in ways that would result in suspicion or distrust. Trustworthiness is vital in our marriage, because it provides stability and consistency to us and our family members.

11. **Truthfulness is** communicating accurately to convey one's best understanding of facts and feelings.

We actively seek to find the truth inside ourselves and share it. When we are clear what is true about ourselves and about our marriage, we can be open and sharing with others. We admit when we make a mistake, and we do not lie about it, even to defend ourselves. We look at the facts, without creating imaginary stories or assumptions about what is occurring. We are clear about when we are expressing opinions and understandings that may or may not yet be proved as factual.

Truthfulness protects us from the damage and destruction that exaggeration, deceit, and lies cause. It is the foundation of our trust in one another. Sometimes we need to draw on courage to speak the truth in a timely and wise way. Truthfulness brings peacefulness to us and builds trust and love. Truthfulness helps the development of all the other character qualities we practice.

12. **Wisdom is** making good choices based upon knowledge gained from careful listening, observation, education, and experiences, as well as through reflecting and determining whether it is best to speak, remain silent, act, or be inactive.

Wisdom increases in our marriage as we learn from one another and mature together. We also learn wisdom from our experiences, mistakes, and problems. We use listening, reflection, discernment, good judgment, experience, and common sense to assess whether our silence, words, or actions will be timely, helpful, and appropriate. Wisdom helps us know when to request assistance, provide advice or input, take action, or be still and silent.

We build wisdom as we seek to see and tell the truth and understand the potential consequences of our words or actions. We specifically seek for wisdom from many sources to guide us. We can learn knowledge and wisdom from both spiritual and scientific sources. We acknowledge our strengths and our limitations. We are truly wise when we are humble enough to admit that no matter how much we strive to understand, there will always be much we do not know.

> (**Note:** More information on these and other qualities are in the books *Pure Gold: Encouraging Character Qualities in Marriage* and *Creating Excellent Relationships: The Power of Character Choices*.)

Couple Consultation Practice: Consider each of these 12 character qualities and consult about how you can individually and together strengthen and apply them. Examples: You could strengthen "flexibility" through making a change in your weekly schedule; at the beginning of a Couple Consultation, you could choose to focus on including the quality of "moderation" throughout.

One Couple's Experience: We both love to be helpful to each other. However, we have learned that it is wise and respectful to consult with each other before jumping in with unasked-for assistance. One particular incident made this understanding clear for us.

We were both working in the yard in different places. I went up the ladder with an electric trimmer and began cutting off branches of a tree. I let them fall down to the ground. My husband saw what I was doing, came over, and began moving around the base of the ladder while gathering up the fallen branches.

Unfortunately, he bumped up against the ladder, which distracted me, causing me to cut the electrical cord with the trimmer. This tripped the power off to our whole home, and I came close to falling from the ladder. "I can't believe you did that! Why couldn't you have waited until I was done?!" I was angry and upset.

Later that day, after we calmed down and we were able to talk about the situation, my husband said, "I'm sorry for getting in the way and causing the accident." I responded with, "I forgive you. And...I'm sorry I yelled at you."

We consulted about what had happened and discussed how to prevent a repeat incident. This helped us realize we had skipped consulting with each other about responsibilities before going outside to work. I was also able to share that it would have worked better for me if we had consulted briefly about the timing of the help before it started.

 Couple Consultation Practice: What did you learn from or appreciate about this story? Is there anything you can apply in your own marriage?

"Looks aren't everything. It's what's inside you that really matters. A biology teacher told me that."

Chapter 5
Including Character Affirmations

GENERATE THE ☼ LIGHT ☼ OF UNITY:
LOVE + CHARACTER + UNDERSTANDING = UNITY

You build unity through using words and tones of voice that nurture love and respect. It often takes many positive comments to balance out even one small negative one or a critical tone of voice. This is especially true if you are interacting poorly in many ways.

To turn a negative pattern around, look for actions you can sincerely praise or affirm. It is especially effective to acknowledge each other using *Character Quality Language*. Here is a list of qualities that particularly apply in marriage to use with this communication tool:

Acceptance	Fortitude	Respect
Assertiveness	Friendliness	Responsibility
Beauty	Generosity	Self-Discipline
Caring	Gentleness	Service
Chastity	Helpfulness	Sincerity
Commitment	Honesty	Spirituality
Compassion	Humility	Tactfulness
Confidence	Idealism	Thankfulness
Contentment	Integrity	Thoughtfulness
Cooperation	Joyfulness	Thriftiness
Courage	Justice	Trustworthiness
Courtesy	Kindness	Truthfulness
Creativity	Love	Unity
Detachment	Loyalty	Wisdom
Discernment	Mercy	
Encouragement	Moderation	(**Note:** Details on all of these qualities can be found in *Pure Gold: Encouraging Character Qualities in Marriage* and *Creating Excellent Relationships: The Power of Character Choices*.)
Enthusiasm	Patience	
Equality	Peacefulness	
Excellence	Perseverance	
Faithfulness	Purity	
Flexibility	Purposefulness	
Forgiveness	Resilience	

With *Character Quality Language*, you acknowledge each other through specifically and sincerely using qualities like those above in your everyday communications. This encouraging practice touches hearts, builds character and relationships, and brings happiness. Here are some simple examples:

- "Thank you for being (Helpful, Flexible, Truthful…) when you…."
- "I appreciated your (Courage, Respect, Patience…) when you…"
- "I love how (Accepting, Enthusiastic, Encouraging…) you are!"

Below are examples that you might say to each other during a Couple Consultation. The first is a positive statement similar to what you may already comfortably make. The second version uses *Character Quality Language* instead, which includes more details.

Example 1:

Focus of Couple Consultation: Weekend activities

Good Statement:
"I am happy that you want to try some new activities with me!"

Better Statement Using *Character Quality Language*:
"I really appreciate how Enthusiastic and Courageous you are being about going water skiing with me this weekend. I know you have not had much experience with being out on the lake in a boat, and I am happy you are willing to try something new with me."

Example 2:

Focus of Couple Consultation: Who will cook breakfast the next day

Good Statement:
"Thanks for being willing to make breakfast."

Better Statement Using *Character Quality Language*:
"It is Thoughtful of you to cook breakfast for both of us before we do the gardening together tomorrow. Thank you for being so Caring. I know you are concerned because I skipped breakfast last weekend and was dizzy."

The first statements are positive, and your spouse will like hearing the words. However, the second, more powerful and specific statements show the spouse is paying close attention, and they more clearly express appreciation.

Using *Character Quality Language* may seem awkward at first, but with practice, you will improve. Having someone notice your use of a quality encourages continued use.

It is often easier to criticize than to see and appreciate what someone does well. It takes practice to look consciously for your spouse's positive actions and speak specifically about them, but it is worth the effort and very affirming for both of you. If you have children, using *Character Quality Language* is also an excellent way to help them build character.

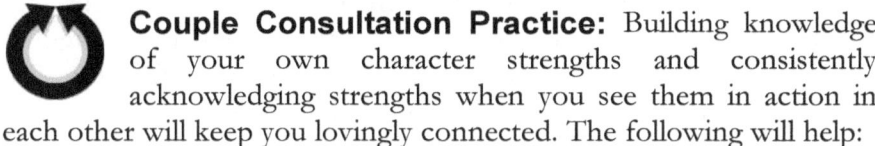 **Couple Consultation Practice:** Building knowledge of your own character strengths and consistently acknowledging strengths when you see them in action in each other will keep you lovingly connected. The following will help:

1. Individually, choose three qualities that you often demonstrate as strengths when interacting with others.
2. Choose one quality to acknowledge in your spouse. Be specific with them about a recent time they practiced the quality and how much you appreciated it.
3. Share about one quality you would each like to strengthen in yourselves. Consult about how to encourage and gently help each other with the growth process.

Deciding in Unity

"The FDA has classified compliments as an essential nutrient."

* "FDA" stands for the US Food and Drug Administration

 **One Couple's Experience:** When we married, my husband owned a house that he and his ex-wife had rented to mutual friends of ours years before. Owning the property was becoming a problem for us, and we had to decide what to do with it. One complication was they had made a verbal agreement that part of the rental payments would go towards the friends' purchasing the house.

As we began to consult, my husband shared, "I'm so frustrated with spending two weekends a month driving 90-minutes round-trip to the house and doing hours of maintenance." I added, "We also need money to pay college tuition." My stepdaughter was headed into a four-year program. Selling the property seemed like a logical choice, but there were complications.

We consulted for weeks. Each time the topic came up, we realized that we were both becoming upset and disunified. I was becoming critical, "Why are you being so difficult about reaching a decision?!" He would push back and react with, "Just leave me alone!" We stopped and waited a few days. This helped us come up with new approaches and ideas for the next time we tried to consult.

Over and over we looked at the issues. What arose as my husband's primary concern was our friendship with the renters. He said, "I think they will have difficulty finding another place to live that would work for them. I'm afraid that we'll lose them as friends." He was concerned they would be angry. He was also certain that he would owe them money, since he was breaking the agreement with them. I said to him, "I feel so frustrated and baffled that *I'm* the one advocating that we need the money for *your* daughter's college expenses!"

What began to emerge was that my husband was very committed to being loyal to the friends, and any action that seemed to be against that character quality was virtually impossible for him to consider. And then the light bulb went on for both of us! We needed to ask our friends, the renters, to come pray and consult with us for solutions. Doing the process by ourselves was causing problems instead of solving them.

To our amazement, within an hour of meeting with them, we had expanded our understanding of their situation, thoughts, and feelings. We quickly came to an agreement that we could all carry out in unity.

I was also able to begin acknowledging my husband: "I appreciate that you are a very loyal person. It not only shows in your friendships, it's also a strength for our marriage."

 **Couple Consultation Practice:** What did you learn from or appreciate about this story? Is there anything you can apply in your own marriage?

Chapter 6
Building Understanding: Physical Arrangements

GENERATE THE ☼ LIGHT ☼ OF UNITY: LOVE + CHARACTER + UNDERSTANDING = UNITY

When you need to decide where and when to consult, consider such possibilities as:

- Sitting across from one another in the kitchen
- Side-by-side on a bench in the back yard
- Walking together in a park
- While doing a task together, such as washing the car or cooking

As you consider locations, think of what will help you avoid interruptions and protect your privacy. As you experiment, you will learn what works well for both of you. You may even notice that changing locations and body positions opens up new creative ideas.

Part of what will affect your choices is how long the Couple Consultation will likely take. You may only need a few minutes to settle the matter. Alternatively, one or both of you may require thinking and processing time, which may lead to periods of silence or pausing the process for awhile.

An additional factor in your location choice may be your level of comfort with direct eye contact. For example, if you are uncomfortable with it, you may prefer to sit side-by-side. It may help you to better understand why men and women often adjust their eye contact and how they interpret it.

Consider the information below based on Paul McWilliams's book *Why Men Won't Talk to Women and What To Do About It* (p. 6) and assess whether it applies in your marriage. He reached general conclusions from his observations, and they may not apply to all couples. Remember that what is being talked about here is not the act of rolling one's eyes in response to sharing, something that communicates disrespect or discounts the other's words.

Deciding in Unity

Giving Direct Eye Contact Usually Means	
For Men	For Women
Demand: "Do This. Agree."	"I'm sharing and listening." "I care."
"I'm right." "I'm standing firm."	Shared feelings and bonding
"It's your fault!" "It's not my fault!"	Openness
Aggression, competition, self-defense	Sincerity, respect

Giving Low Eye Contact Usually Means	
From Men	From Women
"I'm not pressuring you for anything."	Distant, upset, unhappy
"Let's be calm, careful, and not argue."	Feeling rejected, disrespected, unloved
Non-threatening, respectful, non-blaming	Lying, hiding, reasons for anxiety

It is wise to avoid making assumptions and to check out the interpretation you are making about eye contact when it is happening. This can prevent misunderstandings or disunity. For example, if a man looks away because he wants to protect the marriage from anger and conflict, a woman could misinterpret it as not caring. If you understand the reasons behind the body language you each demonstrate, it will be easier to generate unity. You can also more freely try out sitting across from one another!

Couple Consultation Practice: Try out different sitting positions and lengths of time holding eye contact to determine what arrangements work best for you.

Immediate Practice: Sit facing each other, knee-to-knee if you wish, and take turns sharing about something that happened over the previous one or two days. It can be anything that occurred, not necessarily something between the two of you. Part-way through the sharing, shift to sitting side-by side and finish talking about the topic. You can even experiment with sitting back-to-back, with space between you or leaning on one another. Consult about the experiences and your responses.

Next Few Couple Consultations: Talk to one another in a variety of circumstances and using a variety of body positions both with and without direct eye contact. Observe and discuss whether your experiences match the table above. Agree on your preferences related to eye contact and locations for Couple Consultation.

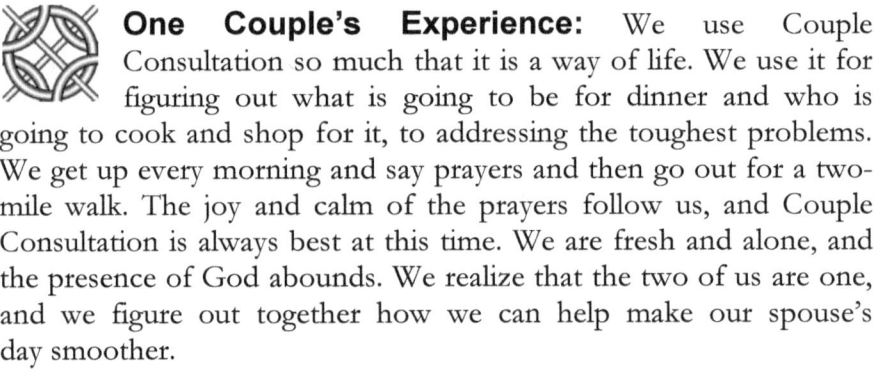 **One Couple's Experience:** We use Couple Consultation so much that it is a way of life. We use it for figuring out what is going to be for dinner and who is going to cook and shop for it, to addressing the toughest problems. We get up every morning and say prayers and then go out for a two-mile walk. The joy and calm of the prayers follow us, and Couple Consultation is always best at this time. We are fresh and alone, and the presence of God abounds. We realize that the two of us are one, and we figure out together how we can help make our spouse's day smoother.

One of the thorniest problems for us to consult through has been infidelity, and obviously our issues were charged and intense. And yet we had to face them and figure out a way to utilize Couple Consultation. A professional therapist had to assist us as well. We needed a big space for consulting, and so we did most of it on walks outside. This gave each of us the chance to say what we needed to say. We had the space and distance to process without having to immediately speak. We were surrounded by nature and by God, and it gave us privacy.

As we walked, we checked in with each other about what feelings were happening, such as whether it was a calm or angry time. Each of us had permission to say that we were not in a space to listen. Each of us had permission to say that we would not speak unless we knew that the other person could hear us. When we began sharing or listening, if our feelings changed, we let the other person know. When we knew the Couple Consultation might be hard and swampy, we often needed warning. This gave us a few moments to prepare to listen for the truth and to listen for understanding.

Once we made the decision to try to work through the infidelity and rebuild our marriage, each of us believed we were acting towards that end. We did our best to give each other the "benefit of the doubt" rather than "assuming the worst." This reduced the possibility of disunity or conflict arising.

Each person's needs were honored, including giving the time to process and understand what the other said. Sometimes this required time alone or bringing up the same point in a slightly different way several times to gain understanding. Sometimes it meant tears to heal, and we gave the space to be sad. We needed time and space for each of us to have our feelings, to grieve, and to forgive.

While Couple Consultation is used to "solve" something, it is also a vehicle to get to truth. We use it to discover our own personal truths by sharing what is going on inside of us. We build our understanding of each other and learn whether we need to make or renegotiate any agreements. Couple Consultation has become a sharing and an integrated way of communicating with each other whether or not problems exist.

 **Couple Consultation Practice:** What did you learn from or appreciate about this story? Is there anything you can apply in your own marriage?

Chapter 7
Building Understanding:
Your Mix of Feelings

GENERATE THE ☼ LIGHT ☼ OF UNITY:
LOVE + CHARACTER + UNDERSTANDING = UNITY

One key aspect of Couple Consultation is discovering and understanding each other's feelings. Your feelings influence how you:

- View the problem you are addressing
- Express your thoughts throughout
- Respond to possible solutions as they arise

Generally, it helps the quality of the Couple Consultation to learn about your feelings early in the process. You also share and try to understand other feelings that arise throughout. If disunity arises, there may be strong feelings occurring to recognize and address.

One challenge with understanding feelings, however, is that you may not yet be skillful with the vocabulary to label them. Marshall B. Rosenberg, PhD, guides people through the challenges of understanding and identifying feelings. He says it's better to avoid using words that express how we interpret communications from others, rather than how we feel, such as:

- abandoned
- ignored
- attacked
- neglected
- misunderstood
- rejected
- unappreciated

He also encourages specificity, which would have you say you are "happy", "excited", or "relieved", rather than saying that you feel "good".

Some of the words you might use for your feelings when your needs are *being met* are:

- Adventurous
- Affectionate
- Amazed
- Amused
- Aroused
- Calm
- Curious
- Energetic
- Fascinated
- Happy
- Mellow
- Moved
- Optimistic
- Proud
- Relaxed
- Surprised
- Thrilled
- Wonderful

Some of the words Dr. Rosenberg suggests for your feelings when your needs are *not being met* are:

- Afraid
- Angry
- Annoyed
- Anxious
- Ashamed
- Bored
- Concerned
- Confused
- Disappointed
- Discouraged
- Embarrassed
- Hurt
- Irritated
- Jealous
- Overwhelmed
- Pessimistic
- Resentful
- Sad

(*Nonviolent Communication, A Language of Compassion*, 2nd Ed, pp. 41-46)

With some practice, you may be able to quickly identify your feelings and name them. Alternatively, you may notice that your feelings only become clear while consulting. You may need feedback and questions from each other to increase your awareness.

Remember to inquire and honor how each other feels, not make assumptions or judgments. It is unwise and likely disunifying to tell your spouse how they feel, to project your own feelings onto them, or to tell them they shouldn't be feeling something.

Your tone of voice is also a powerful cue about your thoughts and feelings. If you listen carefully, you can usually tell if either of you is feeling upset, happy, angry, excited, or annoyed by the tone used to deliver the words. When someone's words and tone of voice do not match, usually you will believe their tone.

As you increase your skill with matching your tones of voice with your words, you will notice that your trust in each other's words increases. When there is trust, you will also find it easier to offer one another gentle feedback and communicate effectively about your concerns.

As you talk with one another about what your different tones of voice mean, you can also explore whether cultural factors, accents, and possibly your unique personalities are affecting communications and causing any misunderstandings.

 **Couple Consultation Practice:** With the help of the lists above, identify both positive and negative feelings that could arise in each of the situations listed below.

1. Your 17-year old daughter drives and has a serious car accident
2. You go out on a date to a concert for your wedding anniversary
3. You burn and ruin a special dinner
4. You take your first vacation in five years
5. You become parents (or grandparents)
6. An incident of your choosing from your lives

To expand your skill in identifying feelings, you can think about different scenarios from your lives, and then practice a few times with saying:

"When I see or hear _____ (or when _____ happens), I feel _____."

If one of you struggles to fill in the feeling, then together you can identify the feelings that can complete the sentence. Be cautious that you don't turn this into a complaint session!

"I do so share my deepest emotions with you! Hungry and tired are my deepest emotions."

One Couple's Experience: When we speak, we are aware of how our words include not only the idea we are trying to convey, but also how we feel about it. With this awareness, we take the time to let our speech be as skillful as it can be, while trusting that the other one will hear us. We speak our minds, and let go of what we have said.

When we listen, we just listen. We are aware of any of our own internal reactions, arising thoughts, and feelings. However, we also know that these have no power when we just open to them and let them be. This allows our minds to stay relatively quiet while the other speaks. We can truly hear what is being said before we form our own opinion and formulate our response.

Our Couple Consultation then, is a process of being aware of our own feelings as we speak and as we listen. There is a sense of great support in knowing that the other is openly aware as we do this. For example, I recently returned home from a week-long business trip. My wife was exhausted from caring for our sick four-year-old son for three days.

When we had a few minutes to sit and catch up with each other and consult about what would happen the next day, we needed time to hear each other's feelings. My wife said, "I was very scared I was going to have to take him to the hospital without you here", and "I was so upset that you didn't call last night to check on us."

I was able to acknowledge her feelings of loneliness and fear about handling this challenge on her own, without jumping into being defensive. She could then hear me as I shared, "I was very frustrated that there was no cellphone signal every place we drove last evening. I was very concerned about both of you and praying for you."

Listening to each other's feelings helped us re-connect. We also realized that we were both too tired to consult about plans for the next day. All we needed right then was to agree on how to look after our son for the next few hours.

 **Couple Consultation Practice:** What did you learn from or appreciate about this story? Is there anything you can apply in your own marriage?

Chapter 8
Building Understanding: Sharing and Listening

GENERATE THE ☼ LIGHT ☼ OF UNITY: LOVE + CHARACTER + UNDERSTANDING = UNITY

One way you build understanding and unity in your marriage is through kind, loving, and effective communications. You share your views, thoughts, and feelings with the goal of harmonizing your purposes and decisions. As you speak and listen to one another with respect, you build a connection of trust and feel safe in the interactions.

You also listen better when you are more concerned about understanding each other than trying to be sure you are heard. There must also be fairness that allows you to be balanced in both listening and speaking.

Practices to remember to use as you talk are:

- Be precise, clear, and pleasant to hear
- Choose a respectful tone of voice and kind language
- Raise concerns without attacking your spouse's character or the character of others
- Reduce criticism
- Avoid coarse, vulgar, or belittling comments
- Stay aware of maintaining equality and unity

Practices to remember to use as you listen are:

- Visualize yourself in your spouse's situation with empathy and compassion. This will help you with better seeing, understanding, and compassionately accepting their perspectives and feelings; recognizing when incidents from the past may be affecting them; and responding when there is some emotional healing to facilitate.
- Truly listen to the words and, whenever possible, understand the emotions and needs behind the words.

- Be relaxed rather than tense to help you focus on the speaker.
- Avoid the tendency to look for ways to "fix" the speaker or situation they are raising and stay focused on the goal of the Couple Consultation.
- Note positive and encouraging words to say in response.

Truly sharing with and listening to one another creates a powerful, intimate bond of trust between you. It:

- Enhances harmony in your communications, helping you feel respected, validated, and appreciated
- Enables you to understand each other's wants, needs, goals, and dreams
- Contributes to your self-respect and self-confidence
- Shows respect and acceptance of each other
- Tells your spouse that you believe they have something worthwhile to say
- Helps your responses be more accurate, encouraging, and helpful

> "Consultation requires the disciplined use of communication skills. The germ of an idea needs to develop through changes resulting from each contribution. The ideal is to produce the best possible results that can be obtained from the minds, the backgrounds, the feelings, and h earts of those participating. Consultation has a p urpose; talking, listening, and communication are the skills which can move an idea toward that objective. Yet no matter how well-developed these skills are, they do not result in consultation if they do not contribute toward the goal."
> ~ John E. Kolstoe, *Consultation: A Universal Lamp of Guidance*, p. 39

Life can become hectic, especially if you have children living at home and both of you work outside the home. When you are going multiple directions, it may often feel as if you communicate briefly, and only what is necessary, to keep your household functioning.

You may also each listen differently. One of you may be able to keep doing a task and still hear well. The other may need more focused attention. Try to slow the pace down enough so that you are sure you are hearing one another. It may be useful for you to have a set time each day to sit and talk.

When you consult, maintain a balance between keeping totally quiet and excessively talking. Encouraging one another to fully share and avoiding interruptions will help you express your viewpoints. Listening allows you to hear each other with both your minds and your hearts without:

- Judging
- Criticizing
- Analyzing
- Planning a response

The truth of the circumstances and best decision emerge when you both participate.

Reflect on your historical roles in communications with each other. Has one of you generally been the talker? If so, then shift your energy to listening more. Has one of you traditionally been the listener? If so, then make an effort to speak more. Welcome a diversity of opinions and perspectives.

Remember to check carefully for understanding as you go along. It is wise to avoid making assumptions or attempting to read each other's minds, which can lead to misunderstandings. Consider summarizing for understanding and also asking key questions, such as, "What is it you think you heard me say?"

Communication experts Susan Heitler, PhD, and Abigail Hirsch, MA, talk about improving the quality of your dialogue and having it feel mutually participatory in four key ways:

1. **Symmetry:** Equalizing voice volumes, your amount of speaking, and speech speed rates; focusing on issues related to each of you
2. **Short segments:** Speaking only a few sentences per speaking time
3. **Specifics:** Giving details and not just generalities
4. **Summaries:** Occasionally reviewing or summarizing the points that have been made

(Based on *The Power of Two Workbook*, pp. 74-75)

As you build awareness of your speaking and listening habits, making adjustments in these four areas may improve your effectiveness.

Loving and Respectful Feedback

Nurture love and respect by encouraging and acknowledging each other's contributions. Here are some possibilities:

- That is a good idea!
- I never thought of it that way before, thank you!
- I appreciate all the effort you put into researching this for us.
- That's an interesting way of looking at this issue. I appreciate the new perspective.
- I can see how committed you are to our marriage and family.

When you disagree with what your spouse says, you can still use love and respect in your communications. Here are some ideas:

- "Hmmm, that's one way to look at it. I have a different perspective…."
- "I'm concerned if we went that direction, what might happen is…."
- "Right now I don't agree with that opinion, but perhaps if you share a bit more information with me, I will understand what you are saying differently."

> "Communicating is giving of ourselves, which is all that we are. Communication is the link necessary to integrate two persons with separate identities into a marriage. The kinds of communication that nourish a marriage are listening with understanding, appreciating and affirming your partner, making requests for what you want, making and keeping promises, and expressing your feelings. These communications will increase intimacy and develop a partnership that will bring out the best in each person."
> ~ Sandra Gray Bender, PhD, *Recreating Marriage with the Same Old Spouse*, p. 87

Deferring to One Another

Even when you consult effectively and lovingly, perhaps even a few times, you may not reach agreement on a solution. Alternatively, one of you may feel strongly about an issue, or has more expertise on it, and the other has no particular view on the matter. One option in these situations is for one of you to consciously choose to defer to the other's opinion. Deferring works best when it includes a sincere wish to carry out the mutual decision in unity.

Warning signs that you are not fully unified in a deferral situation are when you:

- Feel resentment and think you are "giving in" to the other person
- Don't participate in carrying the decision out
- Undermine your spouse's actions related to the decision

If you are struggling with participating in the decision, you may need personal reflection time, perhaps along with prayer or writing down your thoughts and feelings. Sharing with your spouse or a trusted friend may also be helpful in shifting you into a more positive frame of mind and action.

It is wise to re-consult after some time has passed to update one another on the issue and assess what is happening. You may decide to do something different at that point. This analogy may help you: Picture yourselves in a boat on a lake trying to decide where to go. If you row in unity to one spot, you can then determine whether you want to be there or elsewhere. If you sit in the middle of the lake with one of you rowing one direction and the other a different direction, you will make no progress.

There are cautions to consider with deferring:

- Agree on what topics are appropriate for deferring and which ones are not
- Monitor whether you are deferring often, which could be a signal that you are not spending adequate time in Couple Consultation
- Frequent deferrals may be a sign that one of you is being unjustly dominant and the other unwisely passive and not

fully participating. Increasing love, respect, and equality in your marriage will build trust between you, and you can encourage each other to behave in new ways.

Marriage Reflection: What do you create in your marriage when you fully share what is on your mind and in your heart? What do you create in your marriage when you truly listen to one another? What are your thoughts about deferring and when it could be helpful or unwise?

Couple Consultation Practice: Listening effectively is a conscious skill that takes time and practice to improve. If either of you are upset, angry, fearful, or experiencing other strong feelings, this can reduce your ability to listen well. Sometimes, before effective problem-solving can occur, you may help each other release and calm down some feelings.

The following activity will give you the opportunity to share stories from your lives that had an emotional impact. You will practice hearing and understanding a range of feelings in each other. The sharing may also build trust and intimacy between you, particularly if you share stories or aspects of stories that you have never shared before.

1. **Spouse 1:** Share for a few minutes about an incident that happened to you when you were less than 18 years old that was painful, a learning experience, or funny.
2. **Spouse 2:** Share what you heard in the story, and comment on what made you think, touched your heart, or made you laugh. Try identifying what your spouse was feeling at the time the story occurred, and check your accuracy with them. Share your appreciation for their honesty and courage in sharing the story.
3. **Reverse roles** and carry out the activity again.
4. **Consult** about the experience and what you learned from it.

If you need to strengthen your listening skills, it may be helpful to choose a topic to discuss and practice saying small chunks. Summarize your understanding of what you heard back to each other to check for accuracy. It is best to avoid repeating back exactly what each other says, as this is likely to seem disrespectful.

Deciding in Unity

One Couple's Experience: We received the news that close friends of ours were getting a divorce after being married only a few months. We were both concerned about them, but I could tell that my wife was particularly shocked and upset. It had only been a few months since her parents had decided to separate. She reacted to this new circumstance by blending her feelings about both experiences together inside of her.

We had to decide how we were going to respond to the news from our friends. We especially wondered how we might be able to remain friends with them without taking sides. It was a very painful Couple Consultation, and my primary role initially was listening to my wife, accompanying her, and helping her release her feelings and thoughts.

She began by sharing memories of good times we have had with our friends and with her parents, and concerns about both of them. She needed to share anger, frustration, and grief. When she got quiet, I waited for a few moments and then asked, "Is there anything else you need to say?" We repeated that process over and over until she cleared out her mind and heart. Only then could we begin to consult about the actions to take with this new situation.

Couple Consultation Practice: What did you learn from or appreciate about this story? Is there anything you can apply in your own marriage?

"You changed your Facebook relationship status 347 times today. Want to talk about it?"

Chapter 9
Building Understanding: When It's Difficult

GENERATE THE ☼ LIGHT ☼ OF UNITY: LOVE + CHARACTER + UNDERSTANDING = UNITY

It is important that you both have ways of de-escalating and staying calm during the Couple Consultation. For example, you may have a humorous phrase or creative gesture that reduces tension.

You may also simply need a few minutes of sitting quietly together and doing individual reflecting and calming down. Agree ahead of time to call for a pause if it is necessary for protecting your unity.

Lightening Up

It can build unity and calm your Couple Consultation when you have the ability to laugh together and appreciate the humorous aspects of your lives. As one of you shares, laughter can spread to lift the spirits of the other. Laughter is often contagious. However, sometimes one person finds something funny, while the other remains indifferent, or even offended. This can be especially true when you have different cultural, social, or economic backgrounds. It is good to forgive quickly and actively invite types of light-heartedness that make both of you smile and laugh with each other (not at each other!).

Part of the process of building a marriage includes understanding each other's sense of humor. You will also learn each other's vulnerabilities and insecurities and where humor can trigger painful emotions instead of resulting in a positive, unifying response. Sarcasm and criticism, which tend to be cutting and negative words, can cause hurt feelings and disunity, even when delivered with a laugh. Teasing can create light and fun moments between you or be hurtful, so remember to pair it with respect and love. Physical humor such as poking or tickling requires mutual consent to work. When done as a way to dominate each other, it can cause harm.

Pausing As Needed

If your Couple Consultation is in too much difficulty to simply lighten up, you may need to completely stop it for awhile. You can ask yourselves, "What would be useful for us right now?" or "What would have us be successful right now?"

Signals that you will likely find it difficult to reach a decision smoothly can be any of the behaviors listed below. When either of you start doing them, disunity can enter the process, and it may be a signal that it's time to pause. Stopping consulting can help you calm down and re-focus on unity and what is best to do.

Unwise behaviors include when either of you:

- Interrupts frequently
- Forces your viewpoint on the other
- Expresses strong and escalating anger
- Deliberately brings up the other's hurtful "hot button" issues
- Implies or states that one of you is right and the other is wrong
- Has a competitive win-lose attitude
- Insults, blames, or is sarcastic
- Conceals important information
- Dominates in words or tone

- Walks away (unless there is danger of violence)
- Does low-priority texting or answers the telephone and carries on a non-emergency conversation
- Belittles, minimizes, or invalidates the other's points of view or feelings
- Points a finger or uses other aggressive gestures or overly dramatic postures
- Dictates by saying, "you should," "you must," "you have to," or "you can't"
- Issues threats

It is helpful for you to have agreed guidelines for when pausing will likely be required. For instance, you are likely no longer listening and participating effectively if either of you is experiencing a significant escalation of feelings. This may be anger or high anxiety accompanied by physical symptoms, such as a rapid heartbeat or sweating. Letting the symptoms subside for 15-20 minutes will make it easier to re-engage in the Couple Consultation. It may help you to remember to be kind, merciful, and gentle with one another.

Often your pauses will be related to escalating feelings or disunity, but other circumstances are also possible. Family needs may arise, or you may want to seek further information.

If a pause results in one of you leaving the home, be courteous and respectful and provide the information of where you are going and how long you will likely be gone. It is also wise to agree on which of you will reinitiate Couple Consultation and when, and then do so without reminding.

Actions While Pausing

Every person and couple will have their own responses when they need to calm their feelings. Do you just separate and let the feelings burn themselves out? That will at least keep you from hurting each other in some way. However, it is unlikely to improve the process of Couple Consultation. Some people may spend some of the pause time working themselves up further with negative thoughts, feelings, and judgments. This may actually hurt the future Couple Consultation.

You may find it useful to do some type of physical activity separately or together, such as exercising, fixing something, or cleaning. One good use of this time is reflection on what happened inside of you that led to the need for pausing:

- What happened in you that led to negative behavior?
- What were your feelings? Thoughts?
- Were they rooted in your own greed, resistance, judgment, or fears?
- Was your ego involved—did it get bruised by something?
- How might you have handled your feelings more skillfully?
- Would it have been possible to see what was going on as it was happening, and be compassionate for both of you at that time?
- Are there things that you can do now to make this type of behavior or reaction less likely to happen in the future?
- Are there warning signs or remedies that you can identify for preventing future issues?
- Is there a prayer or some simple self-talk that you could use to defuse a situation or feelings as soon as they begin to escalate? For example: "Okay, time to calm down now."

If you have reached an impasse in coming together reasonably, it may be wise for you to find some outside assistance with resolving the matter. Ensure that anyone else you involve is skillful, trustworthy, and will not take sides between you.

When you experience a difficult time reaching a decision and then make one, you may choose to immediately begin carrying it out. You may also determine that it is wise to wait a day and "sleep on it" before acting. You can then fine-tune it the next day with any additional insights that arose overnight.

Remember, too, that you may simply need a rest or fun break because you have been working hard at reaching a decision. You may enjoy heading out for a date, a walk, a game of tennis, a swim, or to the back yard to dig in the garden. You then return refreshed. It may also work well for you to carry out some type of service for someone else, and doing that helps re-focus you. Couple Consultation benefits from looking after your well-being and unity.

Couple Consultation Practice: It may help you prevent disunity or conflict if you have one or two ways of stopping a Couple Consultation or situation from escalating into difficulty. Your "caution" or "stop" signals are likely to be different when you are alone as a couple or when you are with other people. Consult about and agree on a physical signal, cue word, or phrase that will help your Couple Consultation lighten up or stop it from becoming difficult.

If you are unsure what to choose, consider:

- What consistently makes you both laugh?
- What physical movement always distracts you and focuses your attention on your spouse?
- What action would clearly communicate your intention? (There was a television show where the couple's agreed signal to stop talking about something was a tug on the earlobe. However, by the time the spouse noticed the signal, the tugging motion was so exaggerated that it was both funny and inappropriate.)
- What phrase could be said in front of others that would be meaningful for the two of you and not seem strange to others?

Couple Consultation Practice: Under what types of circumstances could it be useful for you to include someone else in your Couple Consultations? Consider:

- A professional? [Consider experts such as a financial advisor, lawyer, teacher, doctor, spiritual advisor, marriage professional...]
- A family member?
- Children?
- A friend?

How could you prepare the person to participate effectively in your Couple Consultation? When might it be *unwise* to include someone? (Consider their age, ability, trustworthiness...)

 **One Couple's Experience:** When my husband and I were going through a very challenging time, it seemed that no Couple Consultation, discussion, argument, or anything, was going to resolve the issues. I learned that when someone believes you have an ulterior motive, or that your opinion is self-serving, it does not matter whether you use reason, scripture, or science. Your spouse cannot listen, because the trust is not there. We were at that spot, where nothing I could say or do mattered, and nothing would penetrate or alter his thinking.

I realized that all I could do was stop talking and pray for my husband to see. After a week or so of holding my tongue and praying diligently, I discovered that it was *my eyes* that began to see differently! As I began seeing things differently, and I began changing, then, and *only* then, did I notice that *he* began seeing our situation differently. It was as if through silent prayer, we met halfway. It was then I learned that sometimes a Couple Consultation needs to be primarily between us and God.

 **Couple Consultation Practice:** What did you learn from or appreciate about this story? Is there anything you can apply in your own marriage?

Chapter 10
Consulting in Unity

GENERATE THE ☼ LIGHT ☼ OF UNITY:
LOVE + CHARACTER + UNDERSTANDING = UNITY

The Couple Consultation process helps you harmoniously make both routine daily choices and vital decisions in your marriage. Be kind and merciful to yourselves and each other when your process is bumpy or difficult.

Couple Consultation is a wonderful and important process to learn, but it is not an easy one to master. It takes repeated practice, and each time is an opportunity to learn. The process tends to be easier when you address issues promptly as they arise, and not wait for them to grow bigger and more difficult to resolve.

MR. AND MRS. BRICKSTONE WILL SOON FIND OUT THAT SMALL IRRITATIONS CAN BECOME BIG ONES.

Suggested Couple Consultation Guidelines

Including the guidelines below will help you gradually implement and improve Couple Consultation in your marriage. You will increase your success in working collaboratively through issues together in an atmosphere of openness, objectivity, and humility.

At the Beginning

1. **Prepare in Advance:** Find or prepare any applicable background information. Accomplish any needed self-care, such as eating or sleeping.

2. **Assess Timeliness and Privacy:** Assess whether it is timely to address the matter. Protect your privacy when appropriate. Consider whether your example of working through an issue is good for others to see, especially your children.

3. **Focus:** Agree on the purpose and refrain from bringing up unrelated issues. Stay aware of your thoughts, views, preferences, requests, goals, beliefs, and feelings as well as any factual details. Avoid manipulating each other or the outcome.

4. **Explore Openly:** Work to understand the depths of the problem. Detach from any particular outcome, and be open to learn. Apply your values and beliefs to the situation. Allow the creative process to develop solutions neither of you planned ahead of time.

5. **Build Love and Unity:** Build your loving and unified connection before consulting. Begin with prayer or another unifying action; incorporate these as needed throughout. Remember that your individual interests are interwoven with the interests of your marriage and family.

Throughout the Process

1. **Include Others:** When needed and appropriate, include other people, particularly those affected by the situation and outcome or who have expert input. Involve children when appropriate for their age, maturity, and the topic. Be clear whether they will only share their views, thoughts, and feelings, or whether they will also be part of the decision-making.

2. **Share and Listen:** Share opinions, perspectives, and ideas frankly, honestly, and respectfully in a moderate way. Invite each other's contributions towards consensus. Search for truth and do not stubbornly insist upon your own views. Listen patiently, attentively, and compassionately, checking for understanding throughout.

3. **Practice Equality, Respect, and Fairness:** Participate equally, with all contributions worthy of respect. Avoid domination, blame, constant complaints, abuse, or threats that would sabotage the process or force a decision to go a certain way. Ensure that you fairly consider each other's perspectives. Do not give or take offense at each other's words.

4. **Search for a Diversity of Solutions:** Share specifically in an honest, calm, courteous, loving, and open-minded way. Welcome both agreement and clashes of differing *opinions*, which can spark the truth and keep you focused on finding solutions. Avoid a clash of *feelings*, which can obscure or hide the truth and cause hurt. Search for new insights and facts and apply any pertinent information to the issue.

5. **Monitor the Quality:** Encourage and affirm each other's positive participation and progress. Pause if serious disunity appears, and do what is needed to calm down and rebalance before re-starting. Be thorough and avoid rushing decisions that need more time.

6. **Release After Sharing:** Release your contributions into an imaginary central area where neither of you "owns" them. They belong to both of you, and you can change them as needed. As you gain new perspectives, you create mutual solutions. [Hint: You may find it helpful to actually put a bowl or other container between you to "receive" your words.]

Deciding in Unity

> "Consultation trains everyone in thinking logically; becoming more articulate; listening more effectively to others and noticing feelings and emotions; discovering creative solutions; including ethical considerations in decision-making; learning to be candid, yet courteous; respecting others, their preferences, and views; and practicing the principles of the new paradigm [for marriage]—equality, cooperation, and unity."
> ~ Khalil Khavari, PhD, and Sue Williston Khavari, MA,
> *Together Forever*, p. 160

Making a Decision

1. **Make a Unified Decision:** Settle matters in harmony and love, and conclude with a unified decision. Aim for the best possible decision for the situation from among the options available, not perfection. Ensure that you assess whether the decision will serve your marriage and family well.

2. **Defer As Needed:** At times you may struggle to find an agreed solution, or alternatively one of you may have more expertise or may not have a strong opinion about an issue. One of you may choose to defer to the other's opinion, which is still a unified decision. You then carry out the decision together.

3. **Seek Additional Help:** If you find it impossible to reach a unified decision, and this is causing disunity between you, seek out sincere, trustworthy people whose judgment and wisdom you respect. This may include family members, friends, or experts. Ask for their input on the issue as a means of helping preserve the well-being of your marriage and family.

Carrying Out the Decision

1. **Share Responsibility:** Commit to carrying out the decision wholeheartedly in unity together. Agree on the best ways to carry out the decision, such as what will be done together and what will be left up to individual initiative and judgment. Proceed with agreed actions with a learning-in-action mindset to discover the merits of the decision.

2. **Set up Support Systems:** Put in place any system of reminders or accountability that you both agree will assist the decision to be carried out smoothly. Examples: calendar notations, cellphone reminders, notes on a bedroom mirror, specific goals with dates, checking in with each other periodically....

3. **Pause for Reflection and Assessment:** Reflect on what is happening and assess any successes, progress, or difficulties. Determine the next stage in carrying out the decision or whether a new one is needed instead. Capture any learning that occurred, but avoid criticism or blame about what happened. Focus on the next best unified actions to take.

Couple Consultation Practice: Explore whether you think it might be possible or difficult to have a formula or a specific set of steps for married couples to consult. Are there any actions or process steps that you want to consistently include when you consult? Are there any parts of the process that become less important when you are consulting about routine family matters?

Couple Consultation Practice: Discuss how to apply the Couple Consultation Guidelines to the family situation outlined below.

Nicole and Jackson are a married couple with two children ages 10 and 14. Both Nicole and Jackson have full-time jobs in the healthcare field, and both volunteer as officers for different community organizations. They are asked by one of their community organizations if they as a couple would be willing and able to plan a 1-day community health fair for about 5,000 people.

One Couple's Experience: I married later in life and gained a young adult stepdaughter with the marriage. Shortly after we married, she contacted us about spending a week with us in our small apartment. My husband would be away at work all day, every day of her visit. I was in a state of panic because of my difficulties communicating with her.

I knew I wouldn't be able to fake it for an entire week! I also knew that things kept inside have a way of blowing up in the worst possible ways. There was no way around it. I had to tell my brand new husband that I didn't want to be alone with his "baby" girl.

I said some prayers and asked if we could consult. He knew it was important, because the word "Consultation" has special meaning for us. We sat kneecap-to-kneecap. I began to cry and said to him, "Honey, I apologize so much, and I know I'm about to disappoint you, but I have to tell you the truth. I am really uncomfortable being around your daughter. I'm just not sure how to manage while she is here."

I thought that this could be the end of us. To my shock and amazement, my dear husband burst out laughing! He, too, had the same difficulty communicating with her, and he, too, was nervous!

It was wonderful knowing that neither of us was alone and could offer comfort and support to one another with the visit, which turned out fine.

It was even more wonderful to learn that no matter how difficult the Couple Consultation, we could each participate in the process. We knew we would be heard, that understanding could be achieved, and that our marriage would be stronger for it. We now have a strong marriage, and Couple Consultation is at its foundation.

 **Couple Consultation Practice:** What did you learn from or appreciate about this story? Is there anything you can apply in your own marriage?

Chapter 11
Putting the Process into Action

GENERATE THE ☼ LIGHT ☼ OF UNITY:
LOVE + CHARACTER + UNDERSTANDING = UNITY

Couple Consultation in marriage is usually quite different than conducting a business or organization meeting, which often proceeds in an orderly way guided by an agenda and chairperson. For Couple Consultation, you are likely in personal surroundings and often quite informal in your interactions. Usually it is just the two of you, and there is no such thing as a majority vote. Couple Consultation often flows naturally in the rhythm and activities of your married and family life.

You will learn the types of environment you both prefer for consulting. You may like walking outdoors or sitting in your living room. You could perch on kitchen stools or stand on your back porch. You may prefer Couple Consultations to happen in an area that is neat and clean. You may like public areas like a restaurant or park, or you may prefer consulting in private.

You might spend only a few minutes together and reach a decision on a topic at hand. The process could be longer as you spend a few days working through pieces of an issue while enjoying a cup of tea after dinner. One couple talks as they play a daily game of dominos, and a decision arrives gradually through multiple interactions. Telephone calls, texts, or emails may add information toward your mutual understanding.

If you are having difficulty communicating or consulting, try setting up a regular, daily time to be with each other. Share what happened during your days, talk about what went well and what did not, and raise concerns and issues that came up for each of you. Remember to share your successes as well as the difficulties. Let the other know if you simply want them to listen, or whether you are asking for their input toward a solution. When needed, work together to address a situation.

Assess how you think your communication flowed that day, what went well and what did not. Have patience with yourselves—this daily attention will help your skills to improve gradually.

Deciding in Unity

You may find it beneficial to agree on major areas of your marriage where you will consult before taking significant action. You can also have some general guidelines about who to include in your Couple Consultations. If your children are old enough, agree on when to solicit their input on issues, and when you will let them participate in the final decision.

One couple listed the topics below as their primary areas for Couple Consultation:

- Religion: worship, study materials, and all associated values and activities
- Money: mine, yours, or ours and how it is utilized
- Parenting: roles, styles, responsibilities
- Family activities
- Home roles and responsibilities
- Recreation together or separate
- Trips/vacations: time together and separate
- Sexual intimacy
- Careers
- Caregiving family members

Couple Consultation Practice: Make a list of the areas in your marriage and family life where you agree to consult with one another before making a decision or taking action.

> "The tone of collaborative dialogue is friendly. Even when the topic is a serious one, the tone still feels cooperative, as if you have placed your problem on a table and the two of you have sat down side by side to try to solve it. You feel that you are confronting the problem together, rather than that you are confronting each other.
>
> "Another tip-off that dialogue is collaborative is that you feel a sense of forward movement as you accumulate shared understanding. Adversarial dialogue feels repetitious. When dialogue is cooperative, with each successive comment you feel movement toward a shared plan of action."
>
> ~ Susan Heitler, PhD, *The Power of Two, Secrets to a Strong & Loving Marriage*, p. 11)

Requesting to consult signals to your spouse that you both need to make time to be together and address an important matter. Using the words "Couple Consultation" gives you common language and signals what skills you will both try to use in the process. How you interact during the process communicates to each other that you value each other's input. Any sign of contempt or devaluing each other will cause disunity. When you talk and listen with the intent of understanding each other, you both contribute to the final outcome. Arriving at a unified decision this way assists you both to take responsibility for the decision and to change it later together if the decision is not working.

As you consult, you will draw on your knowledge of each other's competencies and skills. You will recognize when relying on each other's strengths is useful and conveys respect and value. For example, one couple works together in the garden. The wife has studied plants and how to grow them, so anytime they consult about the yard, they draw on this expert knowledge. The husband is clear that if he insists on doing something without Couple Consultation and collaboration, the result is likely to be unhealthy or dead plants!

As you interact with each other during Couple Consultations you will learn more about your own communication habits and when they cause a problem for your spouse. Perhaps you have a tendency to manipulate, strongly urge a particular outcome, or try to "sell" your spouse on a passionate idea. Maybe you interrupt or get distracted with an electronic device. While you will need to be patient with each other's flaws and efforts, it is also wise to address what will improve your Couple Consultations and devise ways to help each other make progress.

You will also express yourselves differently depending on your personalities. Some people are calm and quiet; others are loud and lively. You will learn over time whether to tone down personality traits if you both agree something is disrupting the flow of the Couple Consultation. For example, one couple learned that the wife's high excitement sometimes pulls decisions certain ways, and they realize this prevents adequate fact-finding or balanced input.

One way you will improve the flow of your Couple Consultations is maintaining your loving friendship. As you regularly share meals, go on dates, talk about how to rear your children, cooperate with the housework, share about your work experiences, do community service, share a spiritual life, and talk about your lives and dreams, you strengthen your friendship. Then when you come together to consult and make decisions, you are not strangers to one another. You like and enjoy each other. You can talk about serious topics with greater ease.

As you continue to expand your toolbox of communication skills beyond those provided in this book, you will also discover that you have the capacity to consult more effectively.

Couple Consultation Reflection: While you are learning ways to consult effectively, and for an occasional check-up afterward, it will be wise to reflect on your skill-building. After you consult on a topic, assess together how well the process worked, using the following questions as prompts:

1. Were we able to listen wholeheartedly to one another?
2. Did we each feel heard?
3. Did either of us interact in a manner that was *not* helpful?
4. What are some listening patterns we want to change?
5. Did either of us withhold information?
6. Was it difficult to be honest with each other about our thoughts and feelings? What might improve that?
7. Were we sensitive to one another's feelings?
8. Did we feel understood?
9. Did we express opinions as contributions, not "the truth"?
10. Did we allow ourselves to be distracted by devices? (Examples: phone, computer, TV...)
11. Did we rush just to make a quick decision?
12. What will we do differently the next time we have to discuss difficult matters like this?
13. Were we able to reach a unified decision peacefully?
14. Are we both committed to carry out the decisions we made?

In addition to assessing specific Couple Consultation experiences, also assess your overall progress in learning the process. Some questions that may assist you with this reflection include:

1. What is working well in our Couple Consultation process?
2. Are there any unskillful patterns, however subtle, that are developing? What would have us be more effective?

Deciding in Unity

One Couple's Experience: We have developed a consistent practice in our marriage of "checking-in" with each other for periodic updates. These help us maintain close connection with one another and assess progress and direction on decisions we have made related to a project, activity, or issue. We gain understanding of each other's thoughts, feelings, desires, or beliefs when we ask key questions (in a respectful tone of voice!). Some of the questions that help us connect are:

- "How are you doing?"
- "What's going on?"
- "What's happening with....?"
- "What unexpected demands are pressing on you that are important for me to know?"
- "What do you need from me, if anything, at this point?"

These consistent updates help us stay emotionally and spiritually connected, make better decisions, and avoid intense disunity or conflict. We are tuned into the pace and important aspects of each other's lives in a light and friendly way. This has been especially important for us with parenting young children and doing home renovation projects.

Chapter 12
Engaging in More Practice

GENERATE THE ☼ LIGHT ☼ OF UNITY:
LOVE + CHARACTER + UNDERSTANDING = UNITY

Throughout this book you have had opportunities to practice your Couple Consultation skills. This chapter will give you additional opportunities to practice, either with provided scenarios or with ones of your own choosing. These activities will help you integrate all that you have learned and see where you can still benefit from more practice.

Couple Consultation Skill-Building

To increase your skill level with setting up a Couple Consultation, carry out this activity below together.

Begin by choosing one from the possible scenarios listed below:

1. Sending a child to nursery school when three-years-old.
2. Whether to take a vacation and where to go.
3. Whether to host an activity at your home.
4. Scenario of your choice.

Think of the scenario you chose, and then answer the following questions:

1. What is the goal of the Couple Consultation/the decision to be reached?
2. What are some of the possible issues involved?
3. What are the potential feelings and needs of the individuals involved?
4. Who else might be affected by or may need to be involved?
5. What personal or family values, beliefs, or expert guidance might apply to the situation?
6. What will help to generate unity during the process?

Couple Consultation Practice: What are two or three of your own marriage or family situations that could benefit from Couple Consultation? Make notes and plan to consult together about items on the list. Begin with a mutually decided topic.

More Skill-Building Practice: Couple Consultation Scenarios

Instructions:
- Choose one of the scenarios below. Consult about it together for about 10 minutes, or until you reach a natural stopping point.
- Use whatever body positions are effective for you.
- Optional: Invite one or two people, perhaps another couple, to observe your Couple Consultations and give you coaching, feedback, and mentoring.
- Afterward, discuss what you appreciated about how you consulted and where you think you need improvement.
- Choose a second scenario, and practice Couple Consultation again with it, focusing on improving your skills.

Deciding in Unity

Scenarios:

1. The wife's brother has asked her to lend him $600 so he can fix his car, which he needs to get to work. He is currently taking the bus, which takes about 90 minutes total each day. The money would come out of the joint checking account, and you as the husband and wife, need to agree about lending the money. The brother did not pay back a $300 loan made five months before. Lending him the money might mean delaying paying off a credit card bill. What are the issues? What are the best options? What do you decide?

2. You are a married couple with two children ages 15 and 17. The 17-year-old son has taken driver's training and has his driver's license. Your 15-year old daughter is looking forward to doing the same. You give your son permission to take your car and drive three friends to a city an hour away for the evening. A half hour after he leaves, you receive a call from the police reporting that they pulled your son over for driving 20 miles per hour over the speed limit. The police want to know whether they should impound the car, and they ask whether you want your son jailed or returned home. You also have to decide on the consequences you will give him. What are the issues? What are the best options? What do you decide?

3. You are married and strict vegetarians. The husband's parents are coming to stay with you for a few days. They are meat-eating cattle ranchers, and do not agree with your vegetarian lifestyle choice at all. Consult about how you will manage this issue during their visit in a way that will maintain family unity and harmony— while also maintaining your health or desired lifestyle. What are the issues? What are the best options? What do you decide?

4. You are married, and the husband is working from an office at home. The wife gets home from work in the late afternoons, and the husband generally calls down from the office to say hello. He then comes downstairs about a half hour later. The wife would like her husband to greet her in person at the door when she arrives, instead. Consult about the feelings and needs each person has and come to an agreement about how to manage the greeting

and connection at that point in the day. What are the issues? What are the best options? What do you decide?

5. Consult about a scenario of your choosing.

 **Couple Reflection:** Assess your experiences with consulting about the scenarios, and reflect on what to apply in your marriage. These questions will help you:

- What will you do to help your Couple Consultations generate the light of unity?
- What will help you make effective decisions using Couple Consultation?

End-Note
Coming Full-Circle Back to Unity

GENERATE THE ☼ LIGHT ☼ OF UNITY:
LOVE + CHARACTER + UNDERSTANDING = UNITY

Signs of Unity and Harmony

Unity is consciously looking for and strengthening points of commonality, harmony, and attraction, as well as working with others to build a strong foundation of oneness, love, commitment, and cooperation.

As a married couple, we focus on finding points of agreement between us, as well as between us and others. We bring people together in love, commitment, and cooperation, drawing on the diverse talents and abilities of all to act for mutual benefit. We regard disunity as destructive to our relationship. We build unity through practicing character qualities effectively with one another. We draw on one another's strengths and abilities.

Deciding in Unity

We use Couple Consultation as an important tool to understand our different viewpoints and reach unified decisions. We recognize that the success of our marriage is more important than the attainment of one person's goals at the expense of the other. We build our unity through practicing respect and fairness with one another. The unity of our marriage is a vital and stable foundation for our children and other family members. It is a force that connects us to people everywhere. It is the bond that keeps our marriage intact, strong, and thriving.

About the Author and Publisher

Susanne M. Alexander is a Relationship and Marriage Educator and character specialist with her education and publishing company Marriage Transformation®. She loves how the process of Couple Consultation strengthens relationships and marriages, and she loves participating in Couple Consultation.

In her life, Susanne has been single, dating, engaged, married, divorced, and widowed. She has been a parent, stepparent, and grandparent. She has also been a child and a stepchild. All of this has given her a diversity of experience to share!

The author's understanding of the principles of Couple Consultation and unity and how they can apply to a marriage relationship are inspired by the teachings of the Bahá'í Faith (www.bahai.org; www.bahaimarriage.net).

Susanne is the author and coauthor of over a dozen books on relationships, character, marriage preparation, and marriage. She is available to clients for couple assessments before and after marriage for compatibility or strengthening. She offers educational coaching, workshops, tools for professionals, and more.

Invitation to Participate

As you practice Couple Consultation and learn more about it through experience, please share your insights. Susanne appreciates an interactive relationship with those who use her materials and books and welcomes your feedback, experiences, stories, and suggestions. You can contact her through the website for Marriage Transformation, www.marriagetransformation.com, and by email at susanne@marriagetransformation.com.

www.ingramcontent.com/pod-product-compliance
Lightning Source LLC
Chambersburg PA
CBHW060341080526
44584CB00013B/870